Certification
Simplified

A Primer for Staff and Volunteer Leaders

MICKIE S. ROPS, CAE

The Center for Association Leadership

WASHINGTON, DC

Information in this book is accurate and consistent with certification industry standards at the time of publication. As research and practice advance, however, standards and best practices may change. For this reason, it is recommended that readers evaluate the applicability of any recommendations in light of particular situations and changing standards.

ASAE: The Center for Association Leadership
1575 I Street, NW
Washington, DC 20005-1103
Phone: (202) 626-2723; (888) 950-2723 outside the metropolitan Washington, DC area
Fax: (202) 220-6439 Email: books@asaecenter.org

We connect great ideas and great people to inspire leadership and achievement in the association community.

Keith C. Skillman, CAE, Vice President, Publications, ASAE: The Center for Association Leadership
Baron Williams, CAE, Director of Book Publishing, ASAE: The Center for Association Leadership
Cover and interior by Troy Scott Parker, Cimarron Design

This book is available at a special discount when ordered in bulk quantities. For information, contact the ASAE Member Service Center at (202) 371-0940.

A complete catalog of titles is available on the ASAE website at asaecenter.org.

Published by Association Management Press, an imprint of ASAE: The Center for Association Leadership

ISBN-13: 978-0-88034-344-2
ISBN-10: 0-88034-344-3

Printed in the United States of America.

10 9 8 7 6 5 4 3 2 1

Contents

Acknowledgements

Many colleagues volunteered to review this guide and provide constructive feedback. Some are experienced certification professionals and others are just beginning to experience certification; both perspectives added great value to the final product. My heartfelt thanks to:

Jacqueline Callahan
Callahan & Associates
Professional Development Consultants

Shannon Carter, MA, CAE
Chief Executive Officer
Competency & Credentialing Institute

Greg Melia, CAE
Vice President, Member Relations and Credentialing
ASAE: The Center for Association Leadership

Bill Scott, CAE
Vice President
Management Solutions Plus

Becky Stein, CAE
Certification Manager
American Public Works Association

Louise Wehrle, PhD, CAE
Manager, Certification Programs
ASM International

Pam Weber, CAE
Director of Certification
Association of School Business Officials International

Preface

Why did I write this book and why do you need to read it? Certification is a complex topic with a lot of information to understand. Being a volunteer leader or staff in certification is a responsibility probably unlike any other you've ever had. You aren't expected to know the intricacies of certification coming in, but should get to know them before you start making decisions. Why? Simply put, bad decisions made by a certification board or staff can have big ramifications—as in bad public relations, angry customers, lost certificants, program failure, and even legal battles.

Reading this book will make you better informed. And, informed individuals make better decisions. I'll cover the certification essentials so that you will be able to make those tough decisions based on knowledge rather than emotion, opinion, or simply what sounds right. This should make your job or volunteer role more effective, enjoyable, and ultimately, should help strengthen your organization's certification program.

After you've read this book, don't file it away. Volunteers, keep it with your board materials. Take it with you to your board meetings— let it be your reference. Even if you understand all the concepts during your first read, still, take it with you. Understanding the concepts and recalling them at the right time are two different things. Staff, keep it near your desk because out of sight means out of mind!

You've likely already noticed that this book is written in conversational tone. This is intentional. There are books out there that discuss some (but not all) of the issues within this book; however, you pretty much have to be a certification expert already to comprehend them, which seems to defeat the purpose. This book is different. It assumes no previous knowledge of certification. If you already know the material, excellent, skip ahead; but if you don't, it's here for you.

Because I live and work inside the United States, this book does have a U.S. focus, but most of the information is applicable to credentialing programs worldwide.

I've laid out this guide using questions I've been asked over the years, supplemented by questions I should have been asked more often!

What are the credentialing options?

Credentialing is most often used as the umbrella term to describe the various types of formal recognition programs, including certification, certificate programs, accreditation, and licensure.

There is no governmental or private agency charged with setting and enforcing *mandatory* credentialing standards. That is both good and bad news. The good is that it allows organizations like yours the freedom to develop credentialing programs when, how, and for whom you want. The bad is that it is incredibly confusing for everyone since the terminology is often applied inconsistently, with certifications called *registration*, licensures called *certification* or *registration*, and plenty of certificates called *certification* (see sidebar).

So, a title alone doesn't really tell you much. You must look at the individual program characteristics to determine what they are. And honestly, even then it may not be clear since many programs are actually hybrids of two or more of the program types.

Understanding the similarities and distinctions of these program types is critical to your role as a leader or staff in certification. Many individuals—applicants, employers, and the public—who you encounter will be confused about the credentialing types and terminology, and you have an important role in educating them.

Here's what you should know about each of the various types of credentialing programs.

Licensure

• Licensure is a process through which a governmental agency (or its designated agent) grants recognition to an individual after verifying that he or she has met minimum criteria, including but not limited to passing an assessment.

• Examples include
  − Licensed Real Estate Agent
  − Licensed Practical Nurse
  − Professional Engineer
  − Registered Nurse

• The goal of licensure is to ensure that licensees have the minimal degree of competency necessary to ensure that the public health, safety, and welfare are reasonably well-protected.

• Licensure is granted by a governmental agency (or its designated agent). Other organizations (associations, as an example) do not grant licensure; however, they often have a role in licensure activities. They may advocate for licensure to be instituted by the governmental agency responsible (including providing model language) and they may collaborate with the licensing agencies during development and administration of licensing.

- In the United States, licensure is granted at the state level. In Canada, at the provincial/territorial level.

- Licensure is mandatory. That is, if a state or province/territory has licensure for a given occupation, an individual in that occupation must be licensed to work in that state/province/territory.

- To become licensed, one usually has to meet eligibility requirements (such as years of work experience) and pass an assessment (usually a multiple-choice test).

- The licensure assessment usually covers a broad scope of knowledge and skills at the entry level (that is, minimal competence to perform the role adequately).

- In order to maintain the license, licensed individuals usually have to meet ongoing requirements (such as continuing education or retesting and renewal fees).

- Licensed individuals are granted use of a designation and associated acronym (for example, "Registered Nurse" and "RN") to denote their licensed status.

- There are other forms of governmental regulation, including occupational certification and registration. Because it's not the focus of this guide, I'll not detail the distinctions here. Depending on your field, it may be important to research the regulatory options and distinctions.

Certification

- Certification is a voluntary process through which an organization grants recognition to an individual after verifying that he or she has met minimum criteria, including but not limited to passing an assessment.

- Examples include:
  - Certified Association Executive (ASAE, Washington, DC)
  - Project Management Professional® (Project Management Institute, Newtown Square, PA)
  - Microsoft Certified Technology Specialist (Microsoft Corporation, Redmond, WA)

- Certification can have varying goals; the most common are to protect the public, advance a profession, identify individuals qualified for a role, and to provide a form of recognition to individuals working in a field or a particular role.

- Certification can be granted by almost any type of organization, although among nonprofits, IRS rulings have indicated that 501(c)(6)s are usually more appropriate than 501(c)(3)s.

- Certification is voluntary. Even when certification is offered for a field or for a particular role, an individual does not need to be certified to work in that field or in that role. Still, certification can become very important. Sometimes certification is written in as a requirement in job descriptions or in requests for proposals. Sometimes certifications earn individuals the right to be considered for a specific position or to earn a bonus or salary increase. But, despite the ramifications of not being certified, certification remains voluntary since an individual retains the right to work in the industry or role for which there is certification.

> Licensure is a legal mandate. Certification is voluntary.

- To become certified, one usually has to meet eligibility requirements (such as a minimum amount or level of training/education and years of work experience) and pass an assessment (often, but not always, a multiple-choice test).

- The certification assessment usually covers a broad scope of knowledge and skills—at entry, specialty, or advanced levels, depending on the target audience and goals of the program.

- Certificants (individuals certified) usually have ongoing requirements (such as continuing professional development or retesting and renewal fees) that need to be met every designated number of years to maintain the certification.

- Certificants are granted use of a designation and associated acronym (for example, "Certified Association Executive" or "Mickie Rops, CAE") to denote their certified status.

- Products, processes, or services can also be certified (sometimes called approved) after having met certain quality or minimum performance standards. Examples include Underwriters Laboratory (UL) Mark (Underwriters Laboratory, Inc., Northbrook, IL) and ISO 9000 certification (International Organization for Standardization, Geneva, Switzerland). This guide focuses on the certification of individuals, not product, process, or service certification.

> **Industry Standards**
>
> There are many industry standards to guide certification program development and administration. See page 35 for a list.

Certificate Program

- A certificate program is a voluntary program in which an organization grants recognition to an individual after verifying that he or she has met minimum criteria, including participation in a training or education program and demonstrating comprehension of the program's learning outcomes by passing an assessment.

- Examples include:
    - Certificate in Organization Management (DePaul University's Institute for Nonprofit Management, Chicago, IL)
    - Certificate of Training in Adult Weight Management (Commission on Dietetic Registration of the American Dietetic Association, Chicago, IL)
    - Boating Under the Influence Detection and Enforcement Certificate (National Association of State Boating Law Administrators, Lexington, KY)

- Certificate programs can be offered by any type of organization— for-profit or nonprofit.

- Unlike certification, which focuses on verifying experience and education/training *obtained elsewhere* and *assessing current knowledge and skills,* a certificate focuses on *educating/training individuals* on intended learning outcomes and then *assessing attainment of those specific learning outcomes.*

- Individuals attaining a certificate usually are not granted a designation or associated acronym (e.g., "Certified Association Executive" and "CAE"), but they may be. Most important is that the designation or associated acronym does not state or in any way imply that certificate holders are certified or licensed.

- There are usually no ongoing requirements to maintain a certificate; thus certificates are more like educational degrees (that once granted are never revoked) than certifications (that have ongoing requirements that if not met are revoked).

- *ASTM E2659-09: Standard Practice for Certificate Programs* and *ICE 1100 Standard for Assessment-based Certificate Programs* are standards that guide certificate program development and administration. Since 2009 the American National Standards Institute has been accrediting certificate issuers based upon conformance to the ASTM E2659 standard. The Institute for Credentialing Excellence is currently piloting an accreditation program based on its own standard.

Accreditation

- Accreditation is a voluntary process through which a third-party organization grants recognition to an organization, system, or program after verifying that it has met minimum criteria, usually including but not limited to demonstration of compliance to established performance standards through a submitted application and onsite review process.

- Examples include:
    - Accredited Healthcare Facility (Joint Commission on Accreditation of Healthcare Organizations, Oakbrook, IL)
    - Accredited Natural Stone Fabricator (Marble Institute of America, Cleveland, OH)

- Accreditation of personnel certification programs (American National Standards Institute, Washington, DC and National Commission for Certifying Agencies, Washington, DC)
- Accreditation of certificate programs (American National Standards Institute, Washington, DC)
- Continuing education provider accreditation (Commission on Dietetic Registration, Chicago, IL and American Institute of Architects, Washington, DC)

• Accreditation can be granted by almost any type of organization; however, nonprofits are the most common program sponsor.

• While academic institution and program accreditations are the most well known, many other business entities and programs are accredited.

• Accreditation is voluntary. However, sometimes the accreditation becomes so important that it appears mandatory. As an example, colleges and universities do not need to be accredited, but there are significant ramifications of not being, such as reduced or no funding, degrees not being accepted by other entities (such as certification boards), etc. Despite the ramifications, accreditation is still voluntary because the organization or program can still operate without it.

Examples of Entities Accredited

Colleges and universities

Certification programs

Association management companies

Hospitals

Clinical laboratories

Natural stone fabricators/installers

Continuing education providers

Childcare centers

Zoos and aquariums

• Accreditation usually has ongoing requirements (such as applications, site visits, and fees) that need to be met to maintain the accreditation.

Now, that's a lot of information; to help sort it out, the following table summarizes the key distinctions among the program types.

Table 1: Credentialing Program Distinguishing Characteristics*

Attribute:	Is a mandatory program	Is a voluntary program
	Licensure	Certification, Certificate Program, Accreditation
Attribute:	Governmental agency is the program sponsor	Any other business entity other than governmental agency is the program sponsor
	Licensure	Certification, Certificate Program, Accreditation
Attribute:	An individual is the entity being recognized	An organization, system, or program is the entity being recognized
	Certification, Licensure, Certificate Program	Accreditation
Attribute:	Requires specific coursework offered by the program sponsor as a component of the program	Does not require specific coursework offered by the program sponsor as a component of the program
	Certificate program	Certification, Licensure, Accreditation

* Of course, there are exceptions!

What are the key differences between certification and certificate programs?

Because there is so much confusion between certification and certificate programs, it's worth a more in-depth look at them. In fact, many groups that believe they have a certification program really have a certificate program, or perhaps a hybrid of the two programs.

The primary distinctions between certification and certificate programs are their purpose and core design. The purpose of certification is to assess current knowledge and skills and identify those who meet the minimum criteria established. In a certificate program, the purpose is to educate or train individuals to achieve specified learning outcomes and identify those who have achieved them.

In terms of design, to conform to the international standard *ISO/IEC 17024 General requirements for bodies operating certification of persons*, a certification program must:

- have ongoing requirements (called recertification or renewal) and a system for revoking when requirements are not met

- not have an integrated learning component offered and/or required by the certifying body

In contrast, to conform to the American National Standard *ASTM E2659-09 Standard Practice for Certificate Programs,* a certificate program must

- have an aligned system of learning and assessment, with the assessment evaluating attainment of the intended learning outcomes; and

- not have ongoing requirements or revocation.

Now, what about those programs that issue a certificate of attendance or certificate of participation? Distributing certificates of attendance following an educational event does NOT a certificate program make! A certificate is simply a document awarded to designate the attainment or completion of something.

So, how are certificate programs different from typical symposia or training programs? The key distinction is that certificate programs are based on a predefined course or curriculum with intended learning outcomes and a measurement of learner achievement of intended learning outcomes. In addition, certificate programs are usually broader in scope and longer in duration than typical continuing education/training programs.

In comparison to college- or university-sponsored certificate programs, organization- or corporate-sponsored certificate programs are usually smaller in scope and shorter in duration. Academic certificate programs often range from 40 to 500 contact hours (often taking one or two years to complete), while nonprofit and for-profit corporate certificates are often 15–30 contact hours and often completed within a few weeks or months.

Table 2: Certification and Certificate Compared

	Certification	Certificate Program
Focus	• Verifying education/ training and experience gained elsewhere • Assessing current knowledge and skills	• Educating/training individuals to achieve knowledge/skills and assessing attainment of them
Components	• Assessment of current competencies • Ongoing requirements	• Course(s) based on intended learning outcomes • Assessment of learner achievement of intended learning outcomes
Attributes	• Designation and associated acronym granted • Can be revoked	• No designation or associated acronym granted, or if one is granted, should not state or imply the individual is certified or licensed • Cannot be revoked

It is important to note my liberal use of the term "usually" and "often." Many hybrid programs do exist in the marketplace (e.g., certification programs that require a training component, certificate programs that have ongoing renewal requirements, etc.). However, before you decide to develop such a hybrid program, it is important to weigh the advantages of a blended program versus the disadvantages, such as the potential for confusing stakeholders and the possibility that a hybrid program would not meet industry standards. As mentioned earlier, there are industry standards for certification programs and certificate programs. The hybrid programs will likely *not* meet either the certification or certificate standards.

What's involved in developing a certification program?

More than you might think! The following are the key tasks in certification program development:

- developing a business plan
- establishing organizational structure and governance
- establishing key staff and operations
- developing the certification scheme
- developing policies and procedures
- developing applications and supporting materials
- securing a legal review

This section is comprehensive since some readers will be staff or volunteers for an organization considering or just beginning a certification program. If your program is already developed, you may wish to skim some of the following.

Developing a Business Plan

Integral to the success of a certification program is proper business planning. Organizations should not launch a certification program (or any new product or service) without thoroughly researching the market and determining the business implications of the new venture. But, the business plan's usefulness doesn't end there. It also serves as an important tool to provide a strategic focus for the program and to monitor the program's ongoing progress towards meeting outlined goals. Many organizations also use the business plan as a key component of a funding request for support of the program.

The following template for a business plan outlines the important elements.

Template Business Plan for a Certification Program

Executive Summary

This section should summarize background to the plan, overall progress of the organization to date in developing and/or implementing a certification program, strengths of the organization and areas for development, the major objectives set out in the plan, and the key milestones and targets that will demonstrate success in the future.

Background

This section should describe the impetus for the organization's investigation of developing a certification program and the progress of the organization to date in investigating and developing the program.

Program Purpose and Goals

This section should explain what the organization is trying to achieve through the certification program, setting out the purpose and goals of the certification program. Guiding principles may be included here or in the next section, depending upon their character.

Certification Program Description

This section should describe the characteristics of the program, including but not limited to:

— Eligibility requirements

- Assessment requirements
  - Assessment delivery mode (e.g., paper and pencil/computer)
  - Maintenance and/or recertification requirements

Market Analysis

This section should summarize the outcomes of market research conducted by the organization. It should describe the market in which the certification program operates, including market size, characteristics, segmentation, and trends in general and the specific segment the certification program will target. It should describe the target market and stakeholders' interest in and perceived value of certification.

Competitive Analysis

This section of the plan describes the competitive forces facing the certification program, including identifying the major competitors and outlining segmentation and differentiation strategies, as appropriate, for the certification program.

Certification-related Products and Services

This section of the plan describes products and services the organization offers to support and/or add value to the certification program, including but not limited to training, study guides, resource books, promotional items (lapel pins, mugs), mailing list rentals.

Marketing Plan

This section of the plan identifies the program positioning, goals, and strategies (including segmenting and pricing).

Operational Plan

Governance. This section outlines how the certification program is governed, including identification of the certifying body and what its relationship is to the parent or broader organization, if applicable.

Staffing. This section outlines the staff, volunteer, and consultant/vendor requirements of the certification program, including a discussion of how the organization ensures it has the appropriate personnel in place with the key skill sets and competencies required to deliver all aspects of the plan.

Physical Resources. This section addresses the organization's current or future need for space and capital equipment.

Financial Resources. This section outlines how the certification program is or will be financed. It should cover:

— revenue and expense assumptions
— financial projections for at least five years
— break-even point
— assessment of whether the long-term financial systems are in place to support the certification program

Some of the assumptions that you'll need to make are the number of individuals applying and number recertifying. These estimates should be based on your feasibility study findings (for new programs) or ongoing market research (for existing programs).

You'll also make assumptions about:

— staff and professional services needed
— fees charged for initial application, certification maintenance, and recertification
— fees charged for other products and services
— funding from other sources
— assessment type and delivery system
— marketing expenses
— office and administrative expenses
— taxes

Your budget will include both initial development and ongoing program costs. Most of your initial development costs are for the research in defining the scope and competencies to be assessed and developing the initial assessment form. Possible sources of expenses include:

— staff salary and benefits
— professional service fees (certification program and testing specialists, lawyers, programmers, graphic designers)
— capital expenditures for software and equipment to support candidate databases and tracking systems

- meeting costs of testing specialists and your leaders/test question writers
- honoraria paid to test question writers (if applicable)

Ongoing costs are primarily for test delivery and administration, but also include ongoing committee meetings and procedures to ensure the assessment is valid, reliable, and fair.

Your primary source of revenue will likely be your application/testing fees. Additional sources include maintenance and/or recertification fees and sales of products or services.

Performance Indicators

This section of the plan should describe how the organization intends to measure success in accomplishing the goals and strategies outlined in this plan. This might be accomplished through identification of performance indicators covering financial, qualitative, and quantitative aspects of the plan. Aspects of the plan that might warrant specific performance indicators might include the following:

- Financial performance
- Candidate volume
- Renewal rates
- Market share of the universe of applicants
- Benefits to sponsoring organizations
- Employer support and endorsements
- Membership increase
- Increased sales of education programs/publications
- Salary surveys
- Consumer or stakeholder awareness
- Stakeholder satisfaction surveys
- Credential cited in bid specifications and governmental grants/contracts
- Credential cited in job announcements
- General media coverage and stories in the trade press
- Empirical data regarding the performance of credentialed vs. noncredentialed individuals/organizations

Action Plan

This section should summarize the actions set out in the business plan along with the timelines and responsibilities for achievement.

Establishing Organizational Structure and Governance

An early and important decision certifying agencies need to make is how the certification program will be organizationally structured and governed. Some certifying bodies are independent and separately incorporated as a nonprofit or corporate entity. Other certifying bodies are a committee, business unit, or subsidiary within a larger business entity. The certifying body may be organizationally structured and governed in a myriad of ways as long as impartiality and objectivity are maintained regarding essential certification matters.

The most clear-cut way to maintain impartiality and objectivity is to establish an independent legal entity, but sometimes that is not desired and/or is not financially feasible. It can get more complicated when the certifying body is part of a larger business entity.

If you are at the stage of designing your governance structure, I urge you to slow down and consider all the options. Once a structure is in place, it can be difficult to change. Refer to the "What are the key concepts in certification?" section on page 39 to review the concepts of authority and independence in decision-making, conflicts of interest, and independence from training, all of which are integral to governance structure design.

The Certification Assessment Scheme

A certification scheme typically has at least three components: eligibility requirements, an assessment, and recertification requirements. Some programs have a fourth component: maintenance. Here are the basics to provide you with an overall understanding of what's involved in a certification scheme.

Scheme Components
Eligibility
Assessment
Maintenance
Recertification

Eligibility Requirements

Most certification programs require that applicants meet minimum standards (also called prequalifications) before they can qualify as official candidates. An applicant's eligibility is generally assessed through a review of a submitted eligibility application and associated documentation.

Typical eligibility requirements include formal education or training, work experience, agreement to abide by a code of ethics or standards, and an application fee. They may also include third-party endorsements, work samples, or other certifications or licenses.

> **3 Es of Certification Eligibility**
>
> Education
>
> Experience
>
> Ethics

It is important that eligibility requirements are linked to the actual needs of the role being certified, not randomly chosen; this concept is often called job-relatedness. It is sometimes tempting for a certification committee to drift towards wanting to recognize excellence rather than competence in a role, and for the eligibility requirements to become unnecessarily high. Requirements should be reasonable and reflect the need-to-have, not the nice-to-have. For example, while you might wish all your certificants have a formal degree, is there any evidence to suggest that it is necessary or that those without one do not perform as well? Use your job analysis study (described later) to collect data on what the population's preparation for the role actually is. Decisions based on actual data are essential to the defensibility of your certification assessment scheme.

Eligibility requirements should not include membership in an affiliated organization or purchase of a training program, study course or guide. It would be difficult, if not impossible, to defend the job-relatedness of an association membership. Plus, requiring the purchase of two different products (certification and membership, or certification and training) can place your organization at risk for claims of violation of the antitrust law (as a tying arrangement). If a certification is sponsored by a membership society, it is okay to charge nonmembers more than members for the certification. The rationale for the price structure is that the society invested in the research and development of the program, supported primarily through member dues. The difference in fees must be reasonable and not so high that it compels membership. (read: it shouldn't coincidentally be the cost of membership!).

Assessment

A certification must include an assessment component. While the most common are multiple-choice tests (MCT), this is not the only option. There are also practical skill-based tests, oral examinations, performance checklists, simulations, and portfolio reviews. The type of assessment chosen should be based upon its appropriateness to the type of knowledge and skills being assessed. For this reason, the assessment type should not be selected until a job analysis is conducted.

So what is this job analysis I keep mentioning? A job analysis is the formal process for determining what the target being certified needs to know and be able to do. It is also sometimes called a practice analysis, task analysis, or role delineation. The job analysis usually includes a study of prospective certificants working in the role to be certified to verify the important tasks, knowledge, and skills needed in that role. The findings of the job analysis form the content basis of the certification's assessment and, as already mentioned, should inform the program's eligibility requirements and the type of assessment utilized.

> **Job Analysis**
>
> A job analysis is the formal process for determining what the population being certified needs to know and be able to do.

As examples, a role that primarily applies a knowledge base (such as an accountant) can appropriately be assessed through a multiple-choice test. However, a role that primarily applies skill (such as a crane operator) would best be assessed through an actual demonstration of crane operation. If you have a driver's license, at one point you had to pass both a written test and successfully demonstrate your skill at driving before you received that license. That's because knowledge of driving alone isn't considered sufficient to demonstrating competent driving.

Maintenance Requirements

Some organizations have requirements that candidates must fulfill on an annual basis in order to maintain the certification. The most common is payment of a maintenance fee that covers ongoing certification services (such as inclusion in an online database, promotion of the certification to stakeholders, identification cards, credential verification services, etc.). Other requirements may include an attestation that the certificant has and will continue to abide by the organization's code of ethics and/or an attestation that the individual has and will participate in professional development, as required for recertification. The maintenance process is usually fairly simple; often a single-page form with payment is submitted by mail or online.

Recertification Requirements

Recertification is an important part of a certification scheme ensuring that certified individuals meet ongoing competency requirements. The length of recertification cycles vary (and is typically dependent upon the pace of change in the role being certified), but is most commonly 3–5 years—that means that certificants must meet recertification requirements for a given period in order to continue to be certified through the next period. If a certificant does not meet the recertification requirements, the certification lapses and he or she may no longer use the credential.

The purposes of the recertification requirements also vary. The purpose of recertification is usually to either *measure* the competence of individuals or to *enhance ongoing* competence. If you want to measure competence, the requirement is usually an assessment—which may have the same (or different) content from the initial assessment. If enhancing the ongoing competence of certificants is the purpose of recertification, the most common requirement is a minimum amount of professional development (sometimes called continuing education, although I find that term limiting since it sounds like formal activities are the only acceptable learning activities). There is typically a fee associated with applying for recertification. Organizations may also have additional requirements, such as documented current or recent practice in the role being certified, references, or agreement to continue to abide by the organization's code of ethics. A growing trend is to allow certificants a menu of recertification options from which they may select. If you allow options, it is important that your recertification purpose drives the options available; in other words, they should be intentional, not random.

Certification programs should not grant a lifetime certification. It is impossible to make claims to the public that certificants are competent if they have only been assessed once, perhaps 30 years ago (or even 3 years ago, depending upon how rapidly a role or industry changes!). A possible exception to this rule is when an organization wishes to allow retirees who are no longer working in the field, the option of paying a nominal fee to remain on the organization's roster as a certified person. Such a status should include an overt indication that the certificant is retired.

Developing the Test

When developing a test, the following steps, at a minimum, should be followed to ensure a measurement-sound and legally-defensible test.

- Conduct a job analysis and validation study to identify the content to be tested.

- Develop a set of test specifications based on the job analysis and expert consensus. The specifications should include the content outline of the exam with the relative proportions of each content area and the cognitive levels of questions delineated.

- Have trained subject matter experts develop and review questions based on the test specifications and under the guidance of a testing specialist.

- Conduct a pilot of the test, and analyze the performance of the questions to determine which are acceptable for use on the actual test.

- Construct the final version(s) of the test that will be delivered.

- Deploy a criterion-referenced methodology (such as the modified Angoff approach or the Bookmark approach) to identify the passing score for the test.

- Analyze and track the performance of the test and each question on the test.

- Make adjustments to the test questions, as indicated.

Staffing and Operations

The key functions of certification that need to be staffed include:

- Marketing
- Application processing
- Candidate tracking
- Certificant tracking
- Appeals and complaints tracking and resolution
- Credential misuse monitoring
- Collateral materials development and printing
- Candidate and certificant communications
- Volunteer management
- Document control
- Records management
- Contract management
- Financial management
- Program improvement and evaluation
- Test development and tracking
- Test passing score establishment
- Test performance monitoring
- Test scoring
- Site coordination and logistics
- Proctor coordination and logistics
- Security

The functions involved with development, maintenance, and administration of the assessment tools are the ones that are most often outsourced. It is usually not feasible for an organization to maintain the extensive expertise and infrastructure needed to develop, maintain, and administer certification assessments—at least not at first.

There are many qualified testing agencies that your organization can contract with to assist with these functions. If budget is tight and/or you feel your organization can handle the infrastructure, there are also independent psychometricians (testing and measurement specialists) who can provide the specialized expertise to develop and monitor the performance of your assessment while your organization handles the logistics, databases, security, etc.

One thing is sure: at least one full-time management staff is needed to manage certification, even when much or all of the test development and administration is outsourced. There is a lot of activity that needs to be coordinated and overseen during a new program's development, and a devoted manager is the absolute minimum you should consider.

While corporate certifications are usually developed by staff, certifications sponsored by professional associations or other nonprofits will also typically involve a large cadre of volunteer leaders and subject matter experts in governing the program and in developing the assessment instrument.

Appendix A includes the *Core Competencies of Certification Professionals*, a document that supervisors or human resource professionals may find helpful in writing personnel job descriptions, or certification personnel may find helpful using as a self-assessment.

Essential Policies and Procedures

It is critical that certifying organizations develop comprehensive policies and procedures (before they are needed!) to ensure fair treatment of all candidates, to safeguard the organization from legal challenges, and to prevent negative public relations.

At minimum, policies and procedures need to be developed in the following areas:

Governance Structure and Function
- Governing body autonomy in decision-making
- Governing body composition and qualifications
- Committees
- Conflict of interest and confidentiality

Certification Assessment Scheme
- Purpose and scope of the certification
- Linkage with job requirements
- Components and criteria (eligibility, assessment, maintenance, recertification)
- Test development

Candidate and Certificant Rights
- Use of certificates, logos, marks, designations
- Confidentiality of candidate information

- Information provided to candidates
- Nondiscrimination

Test Administration and Scoring
- Test administration
- ADA accommodations
- Scoring and score reporting

Candidate Processing, Records, and Security
- Candidate processing
- Candidate registry
- Test security
- Record management and retention

Appeals, Complaints, and Disciplinary Action
- Appeals
- Complaints
- Suspension, revocation, and other disciplinary actions

Management System
- Document control
- Internal audit
- Management review
- Compliance with applicable laws and regulations

Essential Documents

Don't underestimate the time and resources it will take to create, publish, and distribute the written pieces necessary for a certification program. Often, the written pieces are the potential applicant's first and only impression of the program. You want to make it a good one. Here are the key materials that are needed:

- Policies
- Procedure manuals
- Conflict of interest statements
- Confidentiality statements
- Disclosure statements
- Work for Hire agreements
- Promotional brochures

- Candidate handbook
- Eligibility application
- Test application (sometimes eligibility and test applications are combined)
- Retesting application
- Special accommodations request forms
- Score reports and pass/fail letters
- Duplicate score report request form
- Test proctor manuals
- Assessment performance statistics reports
- Financial reports
- Certificates and/or identification cards
- Duplicate certificate or identification card request form
- Fee notices/invoices
- Recertification application
- Requests for proposals
- Contracts

If this seems overwhelming, don't despair. You can find examples of many of these materials online through a search engine (of course you'll need to assess their quality and appropriateness for your situation).

Legal Review of Policies, Procedures, and Key Documents

Certification programs increase the legal liability of the organizations offering them. And, the higher the stakes for a certification program are, the more legal liability is incurred. Certifications are considered high stakes when there are significant consequences placed on the outcome of certification, primarily but not limited to the individual applicant or to the consumer of that individual's services. The following are the two primary determinants of high-stakes certification programs:

- when certification attainment has job-related ramifications (such as when certification is mandated for certain positions or when bonuses, salary increases, or promotions are linked to certification achievement); and/or

- when the role being certified has a high risk of harm to individual or public safety or welfare (medicine, for example).

The next section of this book describes the legal issues in more depth.

What are the key legal issues and how do we avoid them?

Certification programs increase the legal liability of the organizations offering them. This section covers the major areas of legal liability related to certification programs, along with steps you can take to manage such risk.

While these strategies may help to reduce the legal risk posed by certification programs, they do not replace the need to have adequate insurance. Be sure to carry comprehensive general liability, directors and officers, errors and omissions, association professional liability, and (if needed) specialty insurance for certification activities.

This fundamental information should be helpful, but should not be construed as a substitute for legal counsel. Always ask legal counsel to review your organization's policies and procedures.

Antitrust

Certification-related activities that are anticompetitive, discriminatory, based on subjective standards, or implemented without fair procedures are cause for antitrust concern.

To decrease risk:

- Do not disparage other certification programs or individuals not certified.

- Implement fair and reasonable policies and procedures for all applicants.

- Do not require association membership for certification application (although you may charge a reasonably higher fee for nonmembers).

- Establish a separate governing body and maintain authority and autonomy in decision-making from the organization's leadership or other entities if the certification program is housed within a legal entity that conducts other activities.

- Enforce rules prohibiting discussions on salaries and fees at meetings or on electronic discussion lists of applicants or certificants.

- Do not require purchase of a study guide (or other products and services) as part of the certification requirements.

- Monitor volunteers to ensure they comply with these guidelines; the certifying body is responsible for volunteers acting on its behalf.

Common Law Due Process

This area encompasses both substantive and procedural fairness. Substantive fairness refers to using objective criteria that are reasonably related to a legitimate organizational purpose. Procedural fairness refers to the procedures followed in the certification decision-making process. Courts often defer to the professional judgment of the association on substantive standards; procedural standards often come under scrutiny in court because they do not require specialized knowledge of the substance of the certification.

To decrease risk:

- Follow traditionally accepted procedures for test development.

- Use objective criteria for all standards and decisions related to eligibility, application, test scoring, and standard setting. Do not use vague language, such as stating applicants must have "appropriate work experience as determined by the selection committee."

- Apply standards and requirements fairly and equitably. When exceptions are made (such as through granted appeals), document the justification.

- Establish and communicate an appeals process. This process should include, at the minimum, a notice of appeals action, an opportunity to respond, and a consideration of the response by fair and impartial decision makers.

- Establish and communicate a complaints and disciplinary process. This process should include, at the minimum, a notice of complaints action, an opportunity to respond, and a consideration of the response by fair and impartial decision makers.

- Document the rationales for all decisions related to the certification program and its standards; in the minutes, record the motion, who made and seconded it, whether the motion was approved or defeated, and why.

Injury to Third Parties

Also known as tort liability, this refers to a situation in which a certifying body is held liable when a customer suffers harm at the hands of a certified professional. Just consider: One trade association lost a multi-million-dollar verdict when an injury occurred at a facility that held its "seal of approval."

To decrease risk:

- Follow traditionally accepted procedures for examination development.

- Develop standards that are objectively established, evidence-based, and reasonably achievable (indicative of minimal or baseline competence rather than excellence).

- Review and update standards often to ensure they reflect current technology and well-documented practice.

- Do not make exaggerated claims about competency; say only that certified individuals have met the standards of your program.

- Establish requirements for recertification; otherwise, you'd be hard pressed to prove the association has made an attempt to ensure certificants remain qualified.

Confidentiality of Records

During the process of certification, organizations gather information from applicants, candidates, and certificants that is personal, proprietary, or otherwise sensitive. The negligent release of this confidential information could lead to liability for damages under common-law theories, including breach of implied contract, breach of confidentiality, and invasion of privacy.

To decrease risk:

- Develop, publish, and enforce security, confidentiality, and record retention and destruction policies and procedures.

- Keep printed materials in locked, secure areas.

- Password-protect certification-related data on computer systems; only relevant staff should have access.

- Install appropriate firewall protection on computer systems to protect them from hackers.

- Release names of certificants, but never release names of applicants. It is okay for an organization to publish a list of currently certified individuals or to verify by request who is certified. The names of certificants are not confidential; the names of applicants are.

- Have all personnel (staff, contracted and volunteer) sign confidentiality agreements.

- Communicate to applicants, candidates, and certificants the conditions under which records will be released (for example, in compliance with subpoenas).

Intellectual Property

Copyright laws protect original works of authorship, including promotional materials, candidate materials, and test forms. Trademarks protect designations, designation acronyms, and logos. Copyright and trademark registration are not required, but they will give your organization certain legal protections that are not available otherwise.

To decrease risk:

- Conduct a trademark search before deciding on designations, initials, and logos.

- Consider filing trademark registration forms for the designations, initials, and logos you select.

- File copyright registrations on test forms and other certification-related publications. However, do not file your tests the traditional way; otherwise your test will be on file at the Library of Congress! There are special provisions for filing tests in person.

- In all contracts with vendors or subject matter experts, clearly state that they are transferring copyright of produced materials to your organization. Note that works produced by hired personnel automatically transfer copyright to your organization under the work for hire doctrine; works produced by volunteers and consultants do not. You must include a transfer of copyright provision in a written agreement to assure ownership.

Americans with Disabilities Act

Nonprofits are subject to the requirements of the Americans with Disabilities Act (ADA) and must provide reasonable accommodations for individuals with conditions covered under the act. Note that English as a second language (ESL) and attention deficit hyperactivity disorder (ADHD) are not considered disabilities under the act. Therefore, it is up to individual associations to determine if they will provide accommodations for situations like these that are not covered by the act.

To decrease risk, be prepared to comply with ADA by:

- Allocating funds in the certification budget to cover special accommodations requests.

- Asking your testing agency what optional services they can provide (like readers) and the applicable fees.

- Researching vendors, services offered, and fees.

- Not charging the candidate for the accommodations made on his or her behalf; you can account for expenses in the general application fees.

Contracts

In this area, the major concerns for organizations are the terms related to standards of performance, intellectual property ownership, payment, indemnification, and termination.

To decrease risk:

- Spell out exactly what must be done, including deliverables and deadlines.

- Clearly state the ownership of intellectual property. As indicated earlier, ownership is not automatically granted to the organization on materials produced by a consultant.

- Include a clear statement of payment terms, including the maximum fee and payment schedule.

- Include a mutual statement limiting each party's liability to certain terms.

- Note the duration of the contract and termination terms.

How can we assure stakeholders of the quality of our certification program?

Conforming with industry standards is a great way to ensure the quality of your certification program. Many voluntary standards and guidance documents do exist for developing and administering quality certification programs, including:

- *ANSI/ISO/IEC 17024 Conformity assessment—General requirements for bodies operating certification of persons* (2003) American National Standards Institute (ANSI), Washington, DC.

- *Development, Administration, Scoring and Reporting of Credentialing Examinations* (2004), Council on Licensure, Enforcement and Regulation (CLEAR), Lexington, KY.

- *Principles of Fairness: An Examining Guide for Credentialing Bodies* (2002), National Organization for Competency Assurance and Council on Licensure, Enforcement and Regulation, Lexington, KY.

- *Standards for the Accreditation of Certification Programs* (2002) National Commission for Certifying Agencies (NCCA) of the Institute for Credentialing Excellence, Washington, DC.

- *Standards for Educational and Psychological Testing* (1999) of the American Educational Research Organization, American Psychological Organization, and the National Council on Measurement in Education.

- *Uniform Guidelines on Employee Selection Procedures* (1978), Equal Employment Opportunity Commission, Civil Service Commission, U.S. Department of Labor, and U.S. Department of Justice.

Gaining accreditation from a recognized, impartial, third-party accreditation agency can assure your stakeholders of that compliance with recognized industry standards. While the process of applying for accreditation can be daunting, most agencies find it to also be rewarding. Attaining accreditation can reap many benefits for a certifying body, including

- Assuring the public and learner participants/potential participants that a program meets or exceeds a national or international quality standard;

- Meeting regulatory requirements for third-party verification of quality;

- Fostering greater customer trust;

- Adding attention and prestige to a program;

- Serving as a differentiator when there are competing certifications in an industry;

- Increasing participants' knowledge of industry standards;

- Enhancing certificants' credibility for obtaining employment;

- Providing feedback for improvement of policies, procedures, and operations;

- Helping convince administrators or boards of the need to commit resources to maintain a high quality program;

- Assuring the credibility of a program to potential funding sources;

- Keeping program volunteers and leaders knowledgeable of and in line with current best practices; and

- Eliminating the need for duplicative industry certification programs globally (e.g., ANSI/ISO/IEC 17024 is an internationally accepted standard, currently ratified by over 80 countries including the United States).

Each association needs to weigh the value of these benefits against the resources required to achieve accreditation. It's also important to remember that the greatest value of accreditation is often in the process of evaluating and comparing your certification program policies, procedures, and operations against a recognized benchmark and implementing a developmental plan to come into compliance with the standard.

The Accreditors

Currently, certifying agencies serving any industry can seek accreditation of their programs through the American National Standards Institute (ANSI) or the National Commission for Certifying Agencies (NCCA). Some industries (nursing and food safety, as examples) also have their own industry accreditation of certification.

ANSI

The American National Standards Institute (ANSI) administers an accreditation program for personnel certification agencies based on the standard *ISO/IEC 17024: 2003 Conformity assessment—General requirements for bodies operating certification systems of personnel.* The ISO/IEC 17024 international standard resulted from a global standard-setting initiative under the auspices of ISO and was ratified by over 80 countries, including the United States.

The ISO/IEC 17024 international standard covers the entire certification organization, and has requirements for the following areas: organizational structure and governance, development and maintenance of a certification scheme, management system (document control, internal audits, and management review), subcontracting, records control, confidentiality, security, requirements for personnel, certification application, evaluation, decision on certification, surveillance, recertification, and use of certificates and logos/marks.

ANSI's accreditation system follows the accreditation process outlined in the international standard *ISO/IEC 17011, General requirements for accreditation bodies accrediting conformity assessment bodies.* This process includes using specially trained assessors to review documents submitted by applicants against defined requirements, conducting on-site assessments of all applicants, and making recommendations to the ANSI Accreditation Committee, which is responsible for making the accreditation decisions.

Accredited organizations must submit an annual report and undergo surveillance site visits at the first and third years of the five-year accreditation period. At the fifth year, the organization must undergo the full accreditation process described.

NCCA

The National Commission for Certifying Agencies (NCCA) is the accreditation body of the membership society, the Institute for Credentialing Excellence (ICE). NCCA accredits personnel certification programs meeting its *Standards for the Accreditation of Certification Programs.*

The NCCA standard covers the following five core areas: purpose, governance, responsibilities to stakeholders, assessment instruments, and recertification. The area of assessment instruments represents approximately 60 percent of overall requirements.

NCCA's accreditation system includes a desk review by the NCCA Commissioners and the determination of accreditation status by the Commissioners.

Accredited organizations must submit an annual report form attesting to the status of the certification program throughout the five-year accreditation period. Every five years, the organization must undergo the full accreditation process described.

What are the key concepts I need to know?

There are several key concepts that are the foundation of a quality certification program: authority and independence in decision-making, inclusivity and balance, conflicts of interest, independence from training, confidentiality, security, transparency, and fairness.

Authority and Independence in Decision-making

A certifying body must have clear authority for independent and impartial decision-making related to essential certification matters, such as certification eligibility criteria; assessment mechanisms; passing scores; or granting, suspending, or revoking certification. Why? Related bodies may have interests and priorities in conflict with those of the certifying body, and program integrity is jeopardized when those entities influence certification decision-making or practices and unfair or inequitable decisions or practices result.

Following are examples of conflicting interests that could jeopardize a certifying body's or its program's integrity:

- When association members complain that the eligibility requirements are too rigorous or the test passing score is too high, the association's board, with an interest in serving members, may attempt to change or decrease the standards.

- A business unit that sells training to candidates who fail a certification exam may have a financial interest in escalating the passing score to increase demand for the training.

- A professional association with members predominately having a particular academic degree may have an interest in restricting certification to individuals with that specific academic preparation.

- A board of directors or a membership department wishes to promote the certification as a benefit of membership, and therefore wishes to restrict application to members.

If an organization is devoted exclusively to certification, its authority and independence is assumed. However, when certification is but one activity of a larger entity (like an association or corporation with divisions or subsidiaries), the legal entity must delegate authority for essential certification functions and decisions to the certifying body.

Official documents (such as the organization's bylaws or policies) should define the certifying body's authority for essential certification decisions and activities, including the provision for acting without approval by another entity. Where there are exclusions to the authority, these should be made explicit (for example, if another entity, such as the organization's board of directors, approves the certifying body's proposed budget).

Inclusivity and Balance

The certifying body structure and processes should enable input from all stakeholders and interested parties without permitting any one interest to predominate or receive favor. The more inclusive and accommodating the structure is for receiving broad stakeholder input, the greater the likelihood that impartiality will be achieved. To ensure inclusivity and balance, organizations should identify who are the stakeholders of the certification program (as examples, students, certificants, educators, employers, consumers, regulators) and ensure each stakeholder segment has representation on the certification program's governing body. The best way to ensure this representation occurs is to outline the required composition of the certification governing body in the organization's bylaws or charters.

Conflicts of Interest

To maintain impartiality, associations should ensure that individuals or entities do not participate in certification decisions or activities when a conflicting interest is present. Here are some examples:

- A coworker of a certificant filing an appeal with the certifying body would have a conflict in participating on the team reviewing that appeal.

- An individual who conducts test-preparation courses would have a conflict in writing questions for the certification exam.

- An individual who is on the board of a competing certifying body would have a potential conflict in participating on a certifying board.

- An organizational entity that approves or accredits the education or training programs for the industry would have a conflict of interest in identifying the eligibility criteria for the certification.

Impartiality can be maintained through 1) appropriate organizational firewalls, 2) conflict of interest policies, 3) requiring signed conflict of interest statements from all individuals involved in certification activities, and 4) reviewing and addressing potential conflicts of interest on an ongoing basis. Having policies and signed statements is not enough; you must continually monitor and address conflicts that arise. Pointing out a potential conflict is not an easy task, but it is essential to maintaining certification program integrity.

Independence from Training

Probably the worst organizational design is when the certification function is housed within and staffed by a department of education or training. The primary conflict here arises when the organization wishes to develop a course of study leading to or preparing individuals for certification. Several factors should be considered:

- In accordance with industry standards, coursework designed and offered leading to the certification or as preparatory training should not be required.

- If offering a preparatory course, nothing should imply that certification would be easier or less expensive if said course is taken.

- If it is desired to list options for courses meeting eligibility requirements or serving as preparatory training, then all known courses should be listed.

- The certification unit should not disclose to any other entities information about the exam that is not available to all candidates. So, when an education department wants to develop a test preparatory course, they do so based on the publicly available test content outline, not based on any insider information (such as the test questions!).

- Individuals involved in the development or review of the certification exam should not be involved in the development or delivery of any exam preparatory coursework or materials.

- The certifying body should be distinct from any entity that develops or approves training or education pathways to certification eligibility. For example, if your parent organization also accredits degree programs that serve as eligibility requirements, that function should be overseen independently from the certification function.

Confidentiality

The certifying body must safeguard its confidential information. While most certifying bodies have policies and procedures set up to safeguard confidential information from external audiences, fewer consider the internal implications. Much of the information maintained by a certification unit should not be accessible to personnel from other units. Databases holding candidate and certificant information should be password-protected. Relevant offices and file cabinets should be locked. The certifying body should not release any information to other business units that it does not release to candidates or the general public. For example, the names of certification applicants should not be shared exclusively with an education or training department that offers preparatory courses—or to the marketing department that sends the brochures.

Security

Maintaining the security of the test is integral to maintaining the integrity of the certification program. If test questions are exposed through accident or malicious intent, the results of subsequent administrations of the exam are rendered meaningless (in other words, not a true discrimination of test taker proficiency because some candidates may have had access to the test answers) and individuals not qualified can be certified. Some exam materials that should be kept secure include:

- Draft tests and test questions
- Tests during printing and mailing
- Item banks
- Test booklets
- Answer keys
- Statistical analysis of tests

Transparency

The requirements and standards for certification should not be kept secret. Key information about the program should be available and easily accessible to all stakeholders. When the standards are being created or modified there should be an open process to solicit input from all materially affected parties. Additionally, pass rates and other general test performance information should be routinely published on an organization's website or in other routine communications.

Fairness

Certifying bodies should ensure that their policies, procedures, and requirements are applied fairly to all candidates and certificants. Substantive fairness is present when certification criteria are clear, reasonable, objective, and supported by evidence. Procedural fairness exists when policies and procedures are uniformly enforced and followed. Due process, a critical element of fairness, must be afforded to certification candidates and certificants. As an example, when a complaint has been filed against a certificant, the certificant is afforded due process only if provided a notice of the action and provided an opportunity to respond (or be heard) by fair and impartial decision-makers.

What are the key testing terms I need to know?

You'll not have to be involved with certification long before words like psychometrics, content validity, and Angoff are thrown your way. Don't fret. Here's what you need to know to be able to talk the talk (and actually understand what you say and hear). And, don't worry if you don't grasp all of these; what's most important first is that you become familiar with the terminology. The deeper understanding will come.

Psychometrics (pronounced "sigh co metrics") is the field of study concerned with the theory and technique of educational and psychological measurement—often of knowledge, skills and abilities—through instruments such as tests. A **psychometrician** is a person who works in the field of educational and psychological measurement. Usually a psychometrican will have an advanced degree in educational measurement or psychology; however, there are no licensures or certifications for the field, so anyone working in measurement can call him or herself a psychometrician (but, seriously, do you know anyone other than a psychometrician who would voluntarily use that title?).

Your organization likely employs (or contracts with) a psychometrician to ensure your tests are fair, valid and reliable (often referred to as **psychometrically sound**). A **fair** test ensures an equal probability for success by all qualified individuals tested (so, as examples, a test would be unfair if it was written in a way that biased towards or against classes of people or if the conditions under which it was administered were not standardized). Put another way, **fairness** is the extent to which test scores are unbiased. An item is considered **biased** if it discriminates between two or more groups based on factors other than that which is being measured—such as age, socioeconomic status, gender, ethnicity, religion, culture, and institutional or regional differences. Bias is also present if an item stereotypes or otherwise provides inadequate representation of minorities.

One analysis to assess fairness is based on **differential item functioning (DIF**—pronounced "dif"). DIF occurs if test takers of different groups (gender or ethnicity, as examples) with approximately the same knowledge (as measured by total test scores) perform differently on individual test questions. Questions with DIF are identified as potentially unfair and should be further reviewed by a group of professionals to determine if there are identifiable reasons for those differences.

A **reliable** test measures something consistently. However, being reliable isn't enough because a reliable measure is not necessarily valid. A **valid** test measures what it is intended to measure. Consider a ruler. A broken ruler may always under-measure a quantity by the same amount each time (so it is consistent—or reliable), but the resulting quantity is still invalid because it is not measuring what it intended to measure (that is, 12 inches).

Just when you think you have it, let me throw in a twist: there are actually several types of validity. One of the most important for certification exams is **content validity.** For a test to be considered content valid, the content of the test must reflect the knowledge or skill actually required for the occupation or role for which the test has been developed (e.g., accounting). In other words, the test should be based on what individuals actually do, not just what any individual or group thinks they do or wants them to do. A **job analysis** (also called task analysis or role delineation) is a type of study that certifying agencies conduct to identify the actual knowledge or skill necessary for successful performance in the occupation or role. So, conducting a job analysis as the basis of your certification exam is critical to establishing content validity (this will be covered in more detail later).

The findings from the job analysis study are used to develop **test specifications.** These specifications outline the content the test should cover and the relative emphasis it should place on each content area. The job analysis—and the resulting test specifications—ensure the certification assessment accurately reflects what individuals do in a particular job, occupation, or profession.

An early decision for new certification programs is what type of assessment is administered (and this should be made based on the type of content being tested and the goals of the test).

- **Selected-response** (also called objective) questions supply the correct answer, which the test taker must select. True-false, multiple-choice, and matching items are examples of selected-response questions, which are scored objectively, without human judgment. By far, multiple-choice answer examinations are the most familiar and most common type of certification exam.

- **Constructed response** (also called subjective) items require the test taker to formulate a response to a statement or question. Completion/short answer questions and essays fall into this category; their complexity determines whether they need to be scored with human judgment.

- **Performance assessments** (also called **authentic assessments**) require individuals to demonstrate what they know or can do. These include oral presentations, skills demonstrations, and portfolios. All require human scoring.

Norm-referenced tests (NRTs) compare test takers to each other (think ACT, SAT or other standardized achievement tests). The scores are reported as percentage ranks (score equal to or greater than X percent). In contrast, **criterion-referenced tests** (CRT) compare test takers to a predetermined standard. Certification **cut-scores**, the score above which candidates pass the test, should be established through a criterion-referenced approach. If certifying agencies used a norm-referenced approach, that would mean your success on the test would depend upon how well your fellow test takers did (which, um, would not be a good thing)!

A certifying agency needs to establish the cut-score (also called passing score) for its examinations. The general approach to establishing cut-scores is called **standard-setting.** There are several specific methods that can be used; the **Modified Angoff Technique** and **Bookmark Methods** are both commonly used for multiple-choice testing and considered to be defensible criterion-referenced methods. Both rely on the collective judgments of content experts, usually in a face-to-face meeting led by a psychometrician.

But, the cut-score on one version of the test (called a **test form**) can't just be applied to other versions because if candidates take a form of a test that is more difficult than another, they would be at a disadvantage in comparison to others—unless some type of adjustment is made. That brings us to **test equating,** a statistical procedure that detects and corrects for changes in test difficulty across different exam forms. Equating ensures that no matter which form of an exam is taken, candidates will be treated fairly and consistently.

Because of the differences in difficulty and adjustments to the cut-score made through equating, the **raw passing scores** (the number of correct answers needed by candidates to pass the exam) will vary among different forms of the exam. Many groups do not report the raw passing scores. Look at the following hypothetical set of scores by a candidate who had to repeat the exam.

Test Attempt 1	**Test Attempt 2**	**Test Attempt 3**
Pass Score: 75/100	Pass Score: 78/100	Pass Score: 80/100
Your Score: 73	Your Score: 75	Your Score: 80
Fail	*Fail*	*Pass*

Can't you imagine this person complaining that the test got harder (since the pass score went up)? However, in reality, the test became easier (the difficulty of items was lower) so through equating the pass score was raised.

To avoid this confusion and enable candidates to make meaningful comparisons among scores, many groups opt to report **scaled scores** (a raw score that has been adjusted for the difference in difficulty to provide the same standard score for the same level of performance).

Test Attempt 1	**Test Attempt 2**	**Test Attempt 3**
Pass Scaled Score: 220	Pass Scaled Score: 220	Pass Scaled Score: 220
Your Scaled Score: 200	Your Scaled Score: 205	Your Scaled Score: 225
Fail	*Fail*	*Pass*

Do you see how much more palatable this reporting would be?

After the cut-score is established on the test form, you are ready to administer the exam. Selected response (or objective) tests can be delivered in paper-and-pencil format or by computer delivery.

Paper-and-pencil tests may be administered using test forms on which candidates circle or otherwise mark their selected responses, or more commonly, administered using test booklets with scannable forms on which candidates darken in circles to denote their answers.

Page-turners are essentially paper-and-pencil tests that have been transferred to the computer. In other words, they are simply a computerized form of a test.

In the more sophisticated **computer adaptive tests (CAT),** the number of questions administered depends on how quickly a determination can be made regarding the examinee's competence to practice. If a clear pass/fail decision can be made after an examinee has responded to the minimum number of questions, the exam will end. If more information is needed to make the pass/fail decision, the exam continues until the maximum number of questions has been answered.

There are two basic types of computer adaptive tests; they either rank examinees from low ability to high ability (**ability estimation examinations**) or sort examinees into two or more mutually exclusive categories (**classification examinations**). Educational tests usually fall into the first category; the ACT and SAT examinations, for example, measure individual ability as compared to others. Classification examinations are used in certification to differentiate between those who have been determined competent and those who are not.

After the test has been administered, a **test analysis** is conducted. In a test analysis, the performance of the test and the individual items are examined. The type of **analysis** conducted depends upon the measurement model you're operating under: classical measurement theory or item response theory.

In **classical measurement theory,** exams are developed by sampling items from the content the test covers, and each item is assumed to make an equal contribution to the measurement. Scores are calculated simply by counting the number of correct answers. In **item response theory (IRT)** (also called **latent trait theory**), it is assumed that a single latent trait underlies test taker ability. This so-called ability that the test measures could be a broadly or narrowly defined aptitude or achievement. Therefore, the probability of a test taker answering a question correctly is related to the individual's level of the underlying ability. Then, rather than simply counting the number of answers the test taker got correct on a test, an individual's ability estimate is dependent on the difficulty level of the items that the test taker got right.

In classical measurement theory, item difficulty and item discrimination are calculated for individual test items.

The **item difficulty** or "P" value indicates the percentage of candidates selecting the correct answer. Acceptable values are in the 35–90 percent range, and you usually want them concentrated around 50 percent. Items with low values may be too difficult or may indicate results at the chance level (in other words, individuals may be guessing). High values may indicate items are too easy and may not provide useful information at discriminating between qualified and unqualified candidates.

Used to estimate **item discrimination**, the **point bi-serial** correlation analysis shows the strength of the relationship between the right/wrong responses of a test taker and the overall performance on the exam. Selection of the correct response should correlate positively with the high performers on the exam. When it doesn't, this signifies a problem. The point bi-serial correlation ranges from -1.0 to +1.0. A score of -1.0 would mean the largest negative correlation (none of the high performers on the test selected the correct response to a particular question). A score of +1.0 would mean the largest positive correlation (all of the high performers on the test selected the correct response to a particular question). Typically considered acceptable values range from +0.14 to +0.40.

Besides analyzing individual item performance, overall test quality is assessed also. Under Classical Test Theory, the **Cronbach's coefficient alpha** or **Kuder-Richardson 20 (KR-20)** are used to provide estimates of internal consistency of multiple-choice tests (the degree of homogeneity among test items or how well your exam measures a single construct). Both the KR-20 and Cronbach's coefficent alpha ranges from 0.00 to 1.00. The higher the value, the better.

Under Item Response Theory (IRT), the **item characteristic curve** is the foundation of individual item performance. There are two technical properties of an item characteristic curve: difficulty and discrimination. Difficulty of the item is where the item functions along the ability scale—either easy if it functions among the low-ability test takers or hard if it functions among the high-ability test takers and discrimination describes how well an item can differentiate between test takers having abilities below the item location and those having ability above the item locations.

Don't worry, if the last couple of concepts aren't clear—these are some of the most complex of topics you will encounter in certification. Unless you're a psychometrician, you won't be expected to be an expert in them! For now, just be confident in being aware of and having a basic understanding of the certification terminology. As you get more experience under your belt, come back and read this again. It'll all make sense in time.

Which groups are the key organizations in certification?

Here in alphabetical order are the key organizations that have a role in professional certification, as setting certification industry standards, providing education or training related to certification, accrediting certification bodies or programs, etc.

ANSI

American National Standards Institute (ansi.org). ANSI is a private, nonprofit membership federation. Its primary goal is to enhance the global competitiveness of U.S. businesses and the American quality of life by promoting and facilitating voluntary consensus standards and conformity assessment systems and promoting their integrity.

ANSI facilitates the development of American National Standards by accrediting the procedures of organizations developing standards against publicly defined ANSI requirements. It is not itself a standards developing organization. Rather, it provides third-party accreditation against existing standards. ANSI administers two accreditation programs for personnel certifying bodies. One accreditation is for all personnel certification bodies (based on the American and International Standard *ANSI/ISO/IEC 17024:2003 Conformity assessment—General requirements for bodies operating certification of persons*); the other is specifically for certifying bodies that certify food protection managers based on standards developed by the Conference for Food Protection. ANSI also accredits certificate issuers based on the *ASTM E2659: Standard Practice for Certificate Programs* standard.

ANSI is the official U.S. representative to the International Organization for Standardization (ISO) and, via the United States National Committee, also to the International Electrotechnical Commission (IEC). As the United States' official member of the International Accreditation Forum (IAF—described later), ANSI solely represents the United States in accreditation of personnel certification bodies.

ASAE: The Center for Association Leadership

The American Society of Association Executives (asaecenter.org) is the leading provider of learning and knowledge for the association community.

ASAE serves approximately 10,000 associations worldwide representing more than 287 million people and organizations. Through conferences, online learning programs, and seminars, ASAE offers education and training related to association management, including certification.

If you're a member of ASAE, be sure to join the Professional Development Section (no additional dues) since that's the section to which most certification professionals belong and where the certification content is generated. In fact, the Professional Development Council recently developed the *Core Competencies of Certification Professionals* which is reprinted in this guide as Appendix A.

ASTM International

ASTM International (astm.org), originally known as the American Society for Testing and Materials, is one of the largest voluntary standards development organizations in the world, and takes a leadership role in addressing the standardization needs of the global marketplace in many areas.

ASTM International is an ANSI-approved developer of American National Standards. Relevant to certification, ASTM International adopted the international standards *ISO/IEC 17024:2003 Conformity assessment—General requirements for bodies operating certification of persons* and *ANSI/ISO/IEC 17011:2004 General requirements for accreditation bodies accrediting conformity assessment bodies* as American National Standards. They also published the American National Standard *ASTM E2659-09 Standard Practice for Certificate Programs.* They are currently working on an American National Standard for performance-based testing.

ATP

Association of Test Publishers (testpublishers.org). ATP is a private, nonprofit organization representing providers of tests and assessment tools and/or services related to education, employment, certification and licensing, or clinical uses. ATP has four divisions, each focusing on a specific area, including Certification/Licensure, Clinical, Education, and Industrial/Organizational. Members of the Certification/Licensure division include publishers of professional certification and licensure exams, managers of information technology certification programs, and test delivery channel vendors.

IAF

International Accreditation Forum (iaf.nu). IAF is a membership organization composed of approximately 60 accreditation bodies around the world. IAF members accredit certification or registration bodies that issue certificates attesting that an organization's management, products, or personnel comply with a specified standard. The accreditation bodies must operate under ISO/IEC 17011:2004 *General requirements for accreditation bodies accrediting conformity assessment bodies* to be a full member. IAF facilitates accreditation bodies entering into formal agreements to recognize each others' accreditations of certification bodies. Thus, their desired outcome is to standardize what is a quality certification body around the world.

ICE

Institute for Credentialing Excellence (credentialingexcellence.org). ICE is a nonprofit membership organization that provides educational, networking, and advocacy resources for certification organizations. ICE hosts an annual conference and several audio and web seminars each year on a variety of certification topics. Members of ICE can also access its online resource library of template policies and white papers.

ICE has two published credentialing standards: *ICE 1100 Standard for Assessment-based Certificate Programs* and *NCCA Standards for the Accreditation of Certification Programs.*

ICE's accrediting arm, the National Commission for Certifying Agencies (NCCA), evaluates certification organizations for compliance with its *NCCA Standards for the Accreditation of Certification Programs.* The NCCA mission is to help ensure the health, welfare, and safety of the public through the accreditation of a variety of certification programs of organizations that assess professional competency. The NCCA uses a peer review process to

• Establish accreditation standards;

• Evaluate compliance with the standards; and

• Recognize organizations/programs which demonstrate compliance.

PTC

Performance Testing Council (performancetest.org). The PTC is a nonprofit consortium dedicated to innovation in the design, development, and delivery of performance testing. The PTC helps users find tools and technologies for implementing performance tests. Its committee discussions allow participants to share problems and solutions specific to performance testing. Presentations at its conferences showcase new techniques applied to performance testing problems. The PTC focuses on design, psychometrics, and implementation issues of performance-based tests.

Where can I get more information?

This primer has hopefully provided you with a solid base of knowledge about certification. However, there will always be much to learn! Following are some sources that may be helpful to you in your ongoing quest to keep updated.

Industry Blogs
Blogs are easily accessible and are free. For most, you can subscribe to receive new posts by email or through syndication into a feed reader on your desktop. There aren't many blogs primarily covering certification topics, but here are the existing ones that post regularly, at the time of this guide's printing.

- *Beyond Certification* by Mickie S. Rops, CAE. Commentary on taking certification and professional development programs beyond the traditional, beyond the status quo, and beyond your expectations. (msrops.com)

- *Cheating in the News* by Caveon Test Security. Commentary and links on the incidence and prevention of cheating on exams. (caveon.com/citn)

- *Credentialing Talk* by Seacrest Company. A place for credentialing professionals to discuss trends, pose questions, seek advice, and share experiences from organizations that vary in size, scope, and industry. (seacrestcompany.blogspot.com)

Books and Learning Programs

The ASAE bookstore has certification books and an ever-refreshing array of downloadable recordings of sessions of past learning programs. Here is just a sampling of what you can find at asaecenter.org/bookstore.

- *Certification and Accreditation Law Handbook, 2nd Edition.* ASAE, Washington DC. 2004

- Certification Slip-ups Exposed (synch-to-slide recording)

- Capitalizing on Your ROI: Getting the Most From Your Certification Program (Digital Media)

In closing...

You have an important job. Certification can be one of the most powerful initiatives of an organization or industry. It can be a key strategy for helping individuals better position themselves in a competitive marketplace. It can help to protect the health, safety, or welfare of consumers. It can ensure customers have access to qualified service providers. It can create standards of performance for a particular role. It can elevate a profession. It can help to transform entire industries. But the extent to which it can accomplish any of these things depends in part upon the knowledge and skill of those responsible for designing and administering the program: that is you!

This is a responsibility to take seriously. And that you've taken the time to read through this guide to this final sentence is a clear indicator you're up for the challenge!

Core Competencies for Certification Professionals

Core Competencies for Certification Professionals

August 2009

These competencies are general descriptions of the behavior or actions needed to successfully perform the certification function. This document represents the broad certification landscape, not any one particular role. There are many roles within the certification function and the particular mix of competencies needed by role will vary.

Developed and approved by the 2008–09 Professional Development Council led by its Knowledge Committee:

- **Mickie Rops, MAEd, CAE,** Mickie Rops Consulting Inc. (Council Vice Chair, Knowledge Committee co-chair)
- **Bob Moore, CAE,** Institute of Food Technologists (Knowledge Committee co-chair)
- **Connie R. Adamson,** National Association of College and University Business Officers
- **Jeff T. Cobb,** Tagoras
- **Bill Scott, CAE,** The Obesity Society
- **Karen Van Duyse,** Recreational Vehicle Dealers Association

Thanks also to the additional certification industry experts who contributed greatly through their review and feedback on the document:

- **Shannon Carter, MA, CAE,** Competency & Credentialing Institute

- **Tony Ellis, CAE,** National Association of College Stores (Council Chair)

- **Jefferson Glassie, JD,** Pillsbury Law

- **Cheryl Gross, MA, CAE,** American Osteopathic Association

- **Christine Niero, PhD,** Professional Testing Inc.

- **Chris Reidy, RD,** Commission on Dietetic Registration of the American Dietetic Association

- **Roy Swift, PhD,** American National Standards Institute

- **Helen Viksnins, MEd, CAE,** American Academy of Optometry (Council Immediate Past Chair)

- **Pam Weber, CAE,** Association of School Business Officials International

- **Louise Wehrle, PhD, CAE,** ASM International

I. Planning Certification Programs

A. Research and Analysis

1. Identify the need to conduct research to inform certification business decisions or standards development, including but not limited to:
   a. considering all the credentialing options before determining if certification is the appropriate strategy
   b. identifying the market potential for and viability of a certification program or related products or services
   c. identifying regulatory bodies and regulations that may impact the program
   d. identifying characteristics of prospective certificants or other stakeholders
   e. assuring a valid, reliable and legally defensible certification program
   f. assuring the ongoing viability of existing certification programs or related products or services
2. Define the research question/intent (needs assessment, environmental scan, awareness, image, satisfaction, feasibility, competitive analysis, segmentation, job analysis, outcomes evaluation, etc.)
3. Select and implement appropriate research design, methods and instruments
4. Ensure cross-functional team involvement, as appropriate
5. Develop a system to track research data
6. Analyze the data in an unbiased manner
7. Report data in a way that supports decision-making
8. Use the information gained to set priorities; change existing programs, products, and services; and create new ones to accomplish association and certification-specific strategic priorities and business plan

Knowledge Needed:
- Research questions related to certification planning
- Research types
- Research methods and instruments available and the strengths and limitations of each

- Data tracking systems available and the strengths and limitations of each
- Data analysis
- Data reporting

B. Strategy Development

1. Identify department/program strategic priorities that support the certification program's purpose and goals based on market research, internal data, and experience and input from the certification target audience, members, staff, and other stakeholders
2. Develop clear and measurable performance indicators for each strategic priority
3. Develop an implementation plan (tasks required to accomplish the strategic priorities and responsible parties and deadlines)
4. Establish and implement mechanisms to monitor plan progress and outcomes

Knowledge Needed:

- Organization's mission/purpose and strategy (if the certifying body is part of a parent organization)
- Available relevant research and internal data
- Program stakeholders
- Elements of a strategy/strategic plan
- Mechanisms to monitor progress in accomplishing plan

C. Business Planning

1. Evaluate data from a variety of sources (market research, needs assessment, trend monitoring, benchmarking, evaluations) to inform certification business planning
2. Determine expectations for business profitability and sustainability (examples: support and funding, resources, expected break-even, return on investments, return on assets)
3. Develop a business plan for new and existing certification programs, including:
   a. Identifying a certification body's business goals and objectives, and strategies and tactics for achieving these

b. Developing clear and measurable performance indicators for each business plan objective

c. Developing an implementation plan, including tasks required to accomplish plan and responsible parties and deadlines

d. Establishing and implementing mechanisms to monitor plan progress and outcomes

Knowledge Needed:

- Organization's (and/or certification unit's) strategic priorities
- Available market research and internal data
- Relevant stakeholders
- Elements of a business plan (financial projections, breakeven points, and total costs, etc.)
- Mechanisms to monitor plan progress

D. Certification Program Design

1. Identify program target audience

   a. Based on the purpose of and goals for certification

   b. Utilizing data from a variety of sources

2. Identify and validate the content of the assessment through job/practice analysis research

   a. Involving key stakeholders

   b. Using subject matter experts appropriately guided by testing experts

   c. Using industry-accepted practices/methodologies

3. Identify the certification eligibility requirements, maintenance requirements (if applicable), and recertification requirements

   a. Consistent with the program purpose and goals and with the certification target audience characteristics

   b. Involving key stakeholders

   c. Based on data and a sound rationale

4. Identify the certification's specifications

5. Design the certification program's disciplinary system

6. Publish relevant program and assessment design information and components

Knowledge Needed:

- Certification industry standards*

- Data available (such as job or practice analysis, market research, needs assessment, trend monitoring, benchmarking industry competencies, etc.) to inform certification program design

- Key stakeholders of the certification program

- Principles integral to certification design, including transparency, consensus, and balance

- Job/practice analysis methods available and the strengths and limitations of each

- Components of test specifications

- Eligibility requirements available and the strengths and limitations of each

- Recertification methods available and the strengths and limitations of each

- Options related to domestic versus international markets and the strengths and limitations of each

* Key Certification Industry Standards

- *ANSI/ISO/IEC 17024: General Requirements for Bodies Operating Certification of Persons* (2003) American National Standards Institute (ANSI), Washington, DC.

- *Development, Administration, Scoring and Reporting of Credentialing Examinations* (2004), Council on Licensure, Enforcement and Regulation (CLEAR), Lexington, KY.

- *Principles of Fairness: An Examining Guide for Credentialing Bodies* (2002), National Organization for Competency Assurance and Council on Licensure, Enforcement and Regulation, Lexington KY.

- *Standards for the Accreditation of Certification Programs* (2002) National Commission for Certifying Agencies (NCCA) of the National Organization for Competency Assurance, Washington, DC.

- *Standards for Educational and Psychological Testing* (1999) of the American Educational Research Organization, American Psychological Organization and the National Council on Measurement in Education.

- *Uniform Guidelines on Employee Selection Procedures* (1978), Equal Employment Opportunity Commission, Civil Service Commission, U.S. Department of Labor, and U.S. Department of Justice.

E. International Expansion Considerations

1. Assess the need for, purpose of, viability of, and risk of international expansion of your certification program
2. Assess the availability of and access to the necessary infrastructure and resources in the countries/regions you target
3. Assess the implications of international expansion to test delivery options
4. Assess the language/translation options and impact to the integrity of the certification program
5. Assess cultural considerations and impact to your certification program
6. Consider the impact of international expansion to your existing program
7. Determine if you need and/or desire recognition from the accrediting body (of certification systems) in the country or countries you are exploring.

Knowledge Needed:

- Global practices, cultural approaches, and customs as they relate to certification
- Global certification standards, such as *ANSI/ISO/IEC 17024: General Requirements for Bodies Operating Certification of Persons* (2003)
- Global accreditation system for certifying bodies (i.e., International Accreditation Forum)
- International laws as they apply to certification
- International credentialing options, including delivering a domestic program internationally, customizing an existing program for a particular region, or creating a truly global program

II. Development, Delivery, and Maintenance of Certification Programs

A. Development of Certification Policies, Procedures, and Collateral Materials

1. Develop fair and equitable policies and procedures to support the critical areas of certification programs (governance, program administration and management, test development and administration, eligibility, recertification, complaints and discipline, suspension and revocation, rights of candidates, records and document control, information about candidates, compliance with applicable laws and regulations, scope expansion or reduction)

2. Develop collateral materials needed to support the certification program (information available to public, information available to applicants and candidates, general promotional and marketing materials/website)

Knowledge Needed:

- Stakeholder needs
- Certification industry standards
- Usual certification policies and procedures
- Usual certification collateral materials
- Legal implications and risk management strategies

B. Assessment Tool Development and Maintenance

1. Develop the certification assessment(s) that are valid, reliable, and legally defensible
   a. Using subject matter experts appropriately guided by testing experts
   b. According to the assessment specifications

2. Establish the passing score
   a. Using subject matter experts appropriately guided by testing experts
   b. Using industry-accepted practices/methodologies

3. Establish and implement test question and overall test performance monitoring/quality assurance measures

a. Using subject matter experts appropriately guided by testing experts

b. Using industry-accepted practices/methodologies

Knowledge Needed:

- Certification industry standards

- Selection of qualified testing experts appropriate to the type of assessment administered

- Passing score methodologies and the strengths and limitations of each

- Equating methodologies and the strengths and limitations of each

- Test performance monitoring techniques and the strengths and limitations of each

- Legal implications and risk management strategies

C. Delivery of Certification

1. Identify and implement appropriate delivery methods for specific program elements (such as assessments, recertification requirements)

   a. Considering the cost, customer service, and accessibility for the candidates

2. Identify appropriate security measures for delivery of assessments

3. Develop and implement orientation, training, and continuous improvement guidance for proctors and examiners, as applicable

4. Establish and manage site coordination and logistics

5. Establish and manage proctor and examiner coordination and logistics, as applicable

6. Consider environmental sustainability and implications in program delivery

Knowledge Needed:

- Certification industry standards

- Delivery methods available and the strengths and limitations of each (paper-and-pencil-based, computer-based, web-based, performance-based, etc.)

- Extent to which your target audience has reasonable access to the delivery vehicles being considered

• Sustainability options and the strengths and limitations of each

D. Assessment Scoring and Score Reporting

1. Conduct examination performance analysis and key/rubric verification
   a. Using subject matter experts appropriately guided by testing experts
   b. Using industry-accepted practices/methodologies
2. Score examinations
   a. Using industry-accepted practices/methodologies
3. Report scores, pass/fail results, and appropriate information to candidates
4. Implement equating methodologies, if appropriate, to ensure comparability of exam form difficulty
5. Generate a technical report of exam development and administration activities and data

Knowledge Needed:

• Certification industry standards
• Score reporting options and the strengths and limitations of each (examples: scaled scores, raw scores, performance by content areas of the exam)
• Equating methodologies and the strengths and limitations of each
• Test performance monitoring techniques and the strengths and limitations of each
• Elements of a technical report
• Confidentiality and privacy issues related to candidate information
• Legal implications and risk management strategies

III. Risk Management in Certification

1. Develop and implement program policies systems and procedures that minimize the organization's risks of legal liability
2. Consult with legal counsel having expertise in certification to assure that internal and external program systems and procedures are legally defensible

3. Monitor and ensure compliance with applicable codes, laws, and regulations

4. Develop and implement contracts and agreements to govern relationships with vendors and others, within your authority

5. Take action to ensure intellectual property (tests, test questions, etc.) is protected

6. If developing a certification mark, consult with patent and trademark attorney

7. Document program development and operational processes and procedures

8. Maintain appropriate insurance coverage

9. Maintain required documents (articles of incorporation, bylaws, contracts, minutes, etc.)

Knowledge Needed:

- Legal issues associated with the development and implementation of certification activities
- Levels of contract/agreement authority within the organization
- Scope of services required and responsibilities for service delivery
- Essential elements of contracts and agreements
- Intellectual property protection
- Risk management strategies
- Insurance options and needs

IV. Marketing Certification Programs

1. Define the scope of the market and identify target segments and key stakeholder groups in building participation in certification programs

2. Identify unique value proposition, preferred positioning, and distinctive brand for certification programs products and services

3. Consider data and experience gained from market research, needs assessment, trends monitoring, benchmarking, evaluations and strategic planning

4. Develop and implement a marketing plan(s) to support the identified positioning and branding, and promote certification programs, products, and services

5. Identify tasks required to accomplish marketing plan and assign responsible parties and deadlines

6. Establish and implement mechanisms to monitor plan progress and outcomes

7. Develop a tracking system of the marketing data

8. Analyze the marketing data in an unbiased manner

9. Report data in a way that supports decision-making

10. Use the information gained to set priorities, improve existing, and create new programs, products, and services

Knowledge Needed:

- Components of a marketing plan
- Marketing strategies and vehicles available and the strengths and limitations of each
- Market segmentation
- Unique requirements for positioning
- Diversity of the target audience and perceived barriers to participation
- Branding
- Tracking systems available
- Marketing impact report

V. Evaluation of Certification Programs

1. Incorporate the objectives identified in the design phase for the evaluation of certification program products or services

2. Develop and implement evaluation plan(s) using an appropriate evaluation methodology and vehicles

3. Identify tasks required to accomplish the evaluation plan and assign responsible parties and deadlines

4. Establish and implement mechanisms to monitor plan progress and outcomes

5. Develop a tracking system of evaluation data

6. Identify and track benchmarks (examples: candidate demographics, revenue, program evaluation)

7. Analyze the evaluation data in an unbiased manner

8. Report data in a way that supports decision-making
9. Use the information gained to set priorities; improve existing programs, products, and services; and create new ones

Knowledge Needed:

- Various evaluation methodologies available and the strengths and limitations of each
- Continuous quality improvement systems and practices (e.g., management systems, internal audits, etc.)
- Tracking systems available
- Benchmarks

VI. Technology in Certification Programs

1. Continually monitor the market for emerging technology options
2. Evaluate the extent to which available technology options meet the requirements of the certifying body and certification program and meet stakeholder needs
3. Include selected technology options in the business plan and budget, as appropriate
4. Decide whether to outsource selected technology options or perform internally
5. Implement, as appropriate, technology-based options for the certification program
6. Keep current on and conform to, as appropriate, new and changing technology standards relevant to test development, test administration, and documentation requirements for eligibility and recertification/renewal

Knowledge Needed:

- Technology-enabled options for job analysis, exam development, marketing, application submission, test delivery, candidate and certificant tracking, product sales tracking, and the strengths and limitations of each
- Confidentiality and security requirements for certification data
- Implications and pros and cons of handling in-house and outsourcing
- Potential vendors

- Target audience access to and capacity to work with the technologies being considered
- Technology standards as they relate to certification (Americans with Disabilities, SCORM, IMS, QTI as examples)

VII. Relationship Management in the Certification Function

A. Interpersonal Relationships

1. Establish honest, transparent, respectful, and caring relationships with staff, volunteers, and other stakeholders
2. Proactively address conflict and disagreement to productively resolve differences
3. Ensure that diverse perspectives are appreciated and included
4. Protect the confidentiality and privacy of candidates and certificants

Knowledge Needed:

- Conflict resolution
- Effective communication
- Group dynamics
- Confidentiality and privacy

B. Organizational Leadership

1. Provide informed consultation to association staff and volunteer leadership on matters related to certification, within the scope of your authority
2. Communicate certification purpose, goals, products, and services to staff, leaders, and other stakeholders
3. Advocate for new certification or related programs, as needed
4. Recommend and/or take actions based on decisions made in the best interests of the organization and certification program stakeholders

Knowledge Needed:

- Communication strategies
- Organizational skills

C. Strategic Partnerships

1. Identify and target appropriate and potentially effective partnerships in support of the certification program's strategy and business plan

2. Develop and/or implement a system to consider and prioritize possible partnerships, assuring there are no real or perceived conflicts of interest, and protecting the integrity of the certification program and its processes

3. Collaborate with potential partners to establish mutual goals, determine relative strengths and weaknesses,

4. Determine and document the relative responsibilities of each partner, timelines, and financial arrangements

5. Seek legal counsel before finalizing partnership details/agreement/ relationship

6. Monitor the effectiveness of partnerships and determine whether to continue, adjust, or end the agreement, as necessary

Knowledge Needed:

• Association policies and procedures regarding strategic partnerships

• Mission and vision of association

• Mission and vision of potential partners

• Conflicts of interest

VIII. Management and Administration of the Certification Function

A. Staffing

1. Determine and maintain appropriate staff size and composition to accomplish certification program purposes and goals

2. Ensure separation of education and certification staff functions

3. Develop and keep current staff position descriptions

4. Orient new staff to the field, mission, program purposes and goals, unique requirements of certification personnel, and position description

5. Train personnel to specific role/position responsibilities (initial and ongoing)

6. Establish and implement procedures for reviewing the performance of personnel (internal and consultants)

7. Encourage and support staff participation in professional development activities

8. Periodically define and communicate staff goals and expectations

9. Determine need for external consultation/vendor services

10. Manage relationships between staff and consultant/vendor partners

11. Consider and manage the diversity of an evolving work environment and workforce (examples: virtual offices, telecommuting, use of consultants, staff travel, staff of differing generations)

Knowledge Needed:

- Applicable employment laws
- Training and professional development opportunities
- Type of consultative vendor services available and required
- Requests for proposals and selection processes

B. Program and Department Administration

1. Develop the certification program governance system that maintains impartiality and objectivity in all matters related to certification to ensure fair and equitable treatment of all persons involved in certification

2. Develop and/or implement systems, policies, and procedures for administering programs, products, and services, including:
   - Candidate processing
   - Certificant tracking
   - Volunteer management
   - Consultant, vendor, and sponsor management
   - Marketing
   - Candidate and certificant communications

3. Plan, coordinate, and manage meetings of volunteer leadership, staff, consultants/vendors, strategic partners to accomplish program purpose and goals

4. Review programs, products, and services periodically for appropriateness, effectiveness, efficiency, cost, and return on investment (ROI)

5. Conduct ongoing review of governance documents to ensure currency and appropriateness

6. Utilize resources efficiently and creatively to meet certificant and other stakeholder needs

Knowledge Needed:

- Certification industry standards
- Appropriate relationship between certification governance and parent association (examples: autonomy, independent decision-making in all matters related to certification)
- Meetings management
- Robert's Rules or other meeting guide
- Data analysis

C. Financial Management

1. Develop, recommend, implement, review, and manage budgets for certification activities

2. Implement appropriate financial controls (balance sheets, income/expense statements, audits)

3. Develop and implement metrics and tools to monitor and manage financial performance

4. Develop and implement procedures including:
   - committee and subject matter expert fees and reimbursements
   - soliciting and managing sponsorships for certification activities, if appropriate
   - consultant/vendor selection and contracts, fees, and reimbursements

5. Monitor and analyze financial statements periodically and adjust budget and programs accordingly to ensure business sustainability

6. Review programs, products, and services for cost-effectiveness and return on investment/return on assets

Knowledge Needed:

- Organization's policies and procedures regarding financial management and budgets
- Financial management principles
- Tax implications relative to products and services (UBIT) for various organizational structures (applies to nonprofits only)

About the Author

 **Mickie S. Rops** has been helping organizations make the right credentialing decisions since 1997. Much of her consulting work is in educating organizations on credentialing options and guiding them in the decision as to which credentialing program, if any, is the right fit for the challenges they face. She also conducts audits and evaluations of full programs or program components to make recommendations for improvement, and she researches and writes background papers to inform decision-making.

Mickie is a dedicated volunteer and leader for ASAE, ASTM International, and the American National Standards Institute. She led ASAE's Professional Development Council's efforts in developing the new *Core Competencies of Certification Professionals*. Mickie is an ANSI lead assessor for assessing compliance with the *ISO/IEC 17024:2003 Conformity assessment—General requirements for bodies operating certification of persons* standard and the ANSI accreditation of personnel certification programs. She also serves as the lead technical advisor for the American National Standard *ASTM E2659-09 Standard Practice for Certificate Programs*, which is the standard against which the ANSI Certificate Accreditation Program assesses compliance, and serves as ANSI's lead trainer on the standard for accreditation applicants. Mickie was awarded the 2009 Robert J. Painter Memorial Award from ASTM International and the Standards Engineering Society for "outstanding service in a given year in the field of standards."

Mickie's blog, *Beyond Certification* (msrops.com), was the first blog for the credentialing community and was named by Ogilvy Public Relations Worldwide as one of the 10 most influential blogs for the association community. She wrote two chapters in ASAE's *Core Competencies in Professional Development,* which is on the Certified Association Executive Authoritative Literature List. Her *Certification Toolkit,* featuring over 150 certification program administration template documents, has saved associations hundreds of hours of research and writing time. Her guide *Considering Certification?* is receiving overwhelming applause by the certification community as the only guide available to help organizations navigate the difficult decision as to whether they should start a certification program.

As a former association staff executive, Mickie directed several high-profile professional certification and self-assessment programs, managed a national association's professional development efforts for over 75,000 members, and facilitated strategy sessions for national and regional associations.

Mickie's first-hand experience as a certification staff executive, applicant, and board member, combined with over a decade of consulting with credentialing agencies of all sizes and across industry segments, enables her to provide real-world advice that takes organizations and credentialing programs to the next level.

Mickie can be reached at:

Phone: 317-810-0013
Email: mickie@msrops.com
Twitter: mickierops

Index

This index does not include the contents of Appendix A: Core Competencies of Certification Professionals.